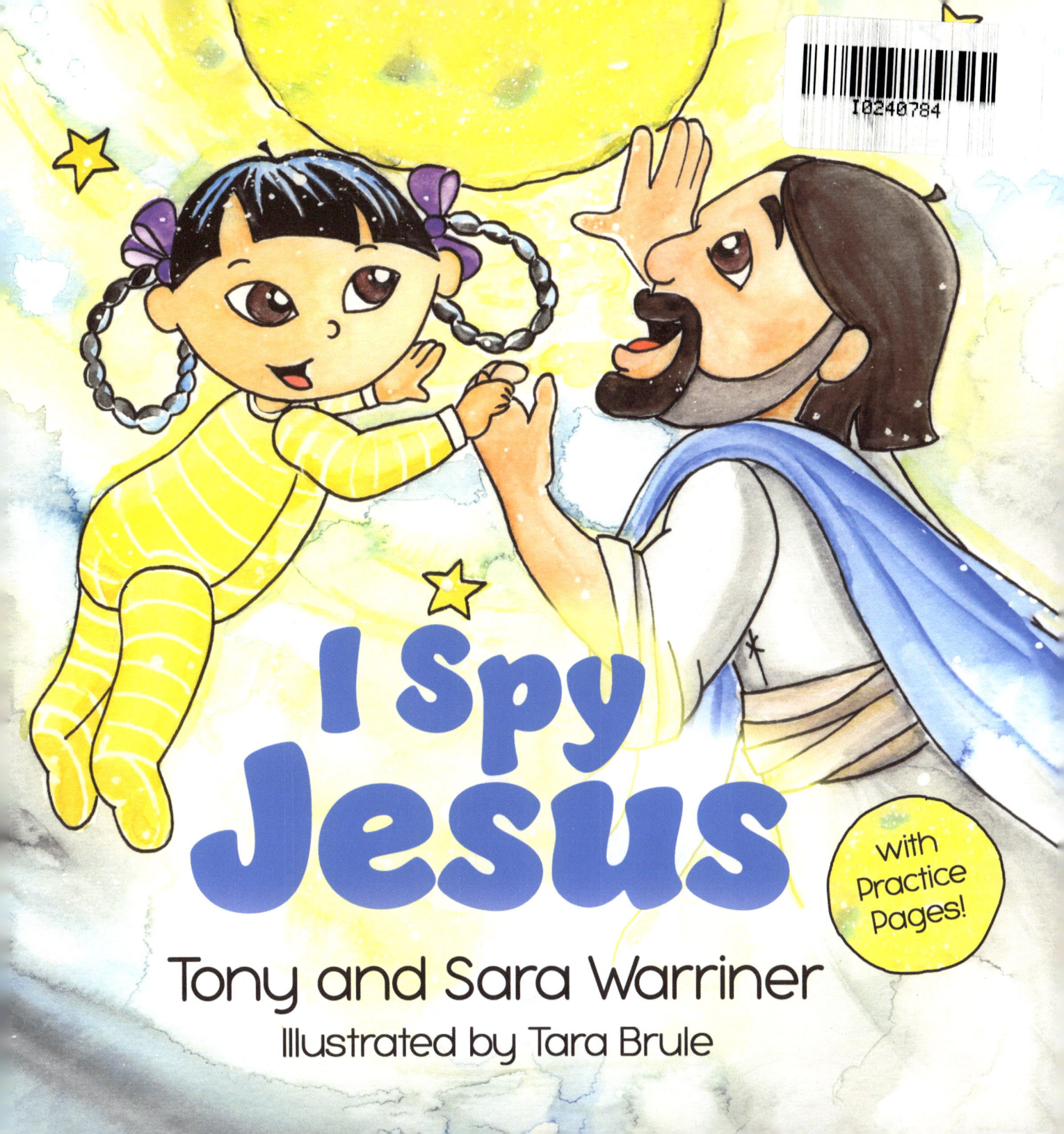

I SPY JESUS
Copyright © 2024 by Tony and Sara Warriner
Illustrations by Tara Brule

All rights reserved. Neither this publication nor any part of this publication may be reproduced or transmitted in any form or by any means, electronic or mechanical, including photocopying, recording or any information storage and retrieval system, without permission in writing from the author.

The STAR tool was created by Church Renewal International. Used by permission.

Scripture quotations are from the ESV® Bible (The Holy Bible, English Standard Version®), © 2001 by Crossway, a publishing ministry of Good News Publishers. Used by permission. All rights reserved. The ESV text may not be quoted in any publication made available to the public by a Creative Commons license. The ESV may not be translated in whole or in part into any other language.

This is a work of fiction. Names, characters, places and incidents either are the product of the author's imagination or are used fictitiously, and any resemblance to actual persons, living or dead, businesses, companies, events, or locales is entirely coincidental.

ISBN: 978-1-4866-2575-8
eBook ISBN: 978-1-4866-2576-5

Word Alive Press
119 De Baets Street Winnipeg, MB R2J 3R9
www.wordalivepress.ca

Cataloguing and Publication information may be obtained through Library and Archives Canada.

We dedicate this book to both
the Warriner children (Luke, Tiana, Jordyn, and Levi)
and the Brule children (Kierra and Kietron),
who are the true trailblazers of inspiration
for the ideas within these pages.

Dear parents,

This book is a tool that will help increase your child's awareness of the very real, everyday, life-changing presence of Jesus. As you read each page, you will find different scenarios that represent various aspects of their lives—from mealtime to playtime, whether experiencing pain or loneliness, or even understanding dreams.

Each scenario has a practice page at the back. These simple exercises will help you and your child experience the presence of Jesus day to day.

Our main focus is two concepts. The first is hearing the voice of Jesus, who made it clear that, as his sheep, we are able to identify when he is speaking to us (John 10:27). Most often he speaks in a whisper or a still, small voice (1 Kings 19:12–13).

The second concept is "seeing" him with the eyes of our hearts (Ephesians 1:18), becoming aware of his presence in our lives. When we behold him, we become like him (1 Corinthians 13:12).

An important note: none of us can claim to hear God's voice perfectly, so our primary safety net is the plumbline of Scripture. If anything we hear or sense in prayer contradicts what the Bible teaches, we disregard it.

Our prayer is that Jesus will lead you and your child into new discoveries of his amazing presence and activity in their lives.

With much love,
Tony and Sara

I Spy Jesus

Tony and Sara Warriner

Illustrated by Tara Brule

I have often wondered what Jesus is like. What he would say? What he would do?

Oh boy, do I have news for you!

Jesus is with me
wherever I go.
Even when I eat,
he's right there I know.

When I'm at church,
Does Jesus see you and I?

Of course he does, friend. He's always nearby!

When I'm having fun, I sometimes forget that there's more going on than I would ever guess.

When I'm at the playground, do you know what I've found?

You guessed it!
Jesus is always around.

Sometimes I fall and it hurts so bad!

What should I do?

I know!

I'll remember that Jesus knows how this feels too.

There are times when I'm all by myself. That's when I pause...

And thank Jesus for blessings and all that he does!

I am learning to see Jesus

everywhere and every day!

When I do, he shows up in unexpected ways.

I love to talk to Jesus whenever I pray!

Even more than that, I love to hear what he'll say!

When it's dark and stormy outside and I feel afraid,

It's important to ask:
What would Jesus do?
What would Jesus say?

Even in my dreams,
when I'm sound asleep,

I Spy Jesus at Mealtimes

Revelation 3:20
Behold, I stand at the door and knock. If anyone hears my voice and opens the door, I will come in to him and eat with him, and he with me.

Teaching Idea for Parents
Jesus deeply desires to be with us in our daily activities. He wants to commune and dwell with us, even during mealtimes. Many of Jesus's most significant encounters with people were over good food (Matthew 9:10-13). Don't miss these opportunities to interact with him!

Exercises for Families
As a symbolic gesture, place an empty chair at your table, acknowledging that Jesus is present and wants to be involved in your daily lives. Imagine what Jesus would say and do as he sits with you. Talk about it around the table. Have fun with this!

Going Deeper
Use prayer before mealtimes to encourage your family to express gratitude and grow in praying out loud. Have each family member take turns expressing thanksgiving. Feeling adventurous? Sing a worship song together. These little moments can be snapshots of momentous praise!

I Spy Jesus at Church

John 10:27
My sheep hear my voice, and I know them, and they follow me.

Teaching Idea for Parents
Be attentive to God's presence while attending events at your local church! The Bible teaches that there is a special grace that comes when we gather with others (Matthew 18:20), whether in worship or prayer, listening to a sermon, or going to Sunday School. Because of this, gatherings can be an effective environment to help your child learn how to hear God's voice.

Exercises for Families
The next time your family is at a church gathering, or even a small group, encourage them to be attentive to what God is saying. Afterward share what you received. Discuss what you felt from this experience.

Going Deeper
Plan a time to do the Whisper Challenge, which is explained at the back of the book. Remember that hearing God's voice takes practice—and the more you practice, the better you and your child will become at it.

I Spy Jesus at the Mall

James 1:17
Every good gift and every perfect gift is from above, coming down from the Father of lights...

Teaching Idea for Parents
Teach your child that Jesus delights in blessing them with good things (2 Corinthians 9:8). His generosity to his children knows no bounds, and he knows their deepest desires. Help your child connect both common provision (like food and shelter) and special blessings (like getting a kiddie ride at the mall) to God's provision.

Exercises for Families
Think of a time when Jesus provided for your family at just the right moment. Recall instances when you were pleasantly surprised by a gift or an encouraging word from someone. Share these experiences together, nurturing a sense of gratitude.

Going Deeper
Let's listen for the whisper of God's voice! Ask Jesus if there's a particular area he would like your family to be grateful for. Your child may gravitate to material possessions, which is a good start, but coach them toward other areas as well, like specific people, past events, miracles, answered prayer, or even difficult challenges. God works in those areas, too!

I Spy Jesus with My Friends

Matthew 18:20
For where two or three are gathered in my name, there am I among them.

Teaching Idea for Parents
It's easy to lose sight of Jesus's presence when we're with others. That's simply human nature! Here's the truth: Jesus is with your child in social settings (such as during play, conflicts, and decision-making) to guide, equip, and grant them wisdom. Help your child learn to live in awareness of this! It can and will save much heartache and difficulty throughout their lifetime.

Exercises for Families
Summarize the story of Jesus appearing to the two disciples on the road to Emmaus (Luke 24:13–35). At first, the disciples didn't recognize Jesus. This is noteworthy, considering they knew him very well in other settings! Come up with a few ideas for how your child can become more conscious of Jesus's presence when they are with friends. Think of this in light of various settings, including school and playtime.

Going Deeper
Think of a time when something positive (or negative) happened with your child when they were hanging out with friends. Consider what Jesus may have been doing or saying in that experience. Listen to his whisper to help you discern.

I Spy Jesus When I'm Hurt

Matthew 10:29-31
Are not two sparrows sold for a penny? And not one of them will fall to the ground apart from your Father. But even the hairs of your head are all numbered. Fear not, therefore; you are of more value than many sparrows.

Teaching Idea for Parents
Jesus is present during difficult times, close to the broken-hearted. Some rightfully say that God speaks most clearly in and through times of heartache and pain, if we have ears to hear and eyes to see. Instill in your child the knowledge that Jesus is with us (and wants to speak to us) in our suffering and that he is a compassionate God!

Exercises for Families
Take time to read the story of Lazarus's death in John 11:33–36. Reflect on the emotions and compassion Jesus displayed in that situation. Discuss with your family the significance of Jesus's presence and empathy during times of hardship and how he brings comfort and hope to us, too.

Going Deeper
For this day, later in the book, we've included a bonus activity for God's Comfort Box. Plan for some extra time for assembly.

I Spy Jesus When I'm By Myself

Philippians 4:6-7
…do not be anxious about anything, but in everything by prayer and supplication with thanksgiving let your requests be made known to God. And the peace of God, which surpasses all understanding, will guard your hearts and your minds in Christ Jesus.

Teaching Idea for Parents
There is a helpful tool called STAR that you can use to navigate different emotions and situations. Use it anytime your child is feeling anxious, alone, afraid, happy, or sad. STAR stands for:
- *Stop* what you are doing. Be still (Psalm 46:10).
- *Take* a big, deep breath (or two). This helps you quiet yourself.
- *Appreciate* Jesus for who he is and what he has done.
- *Respond* by being attentive to Jesus's presence. What is he saying or doing? What is he asking you to do?

Exercises for Families
Practice using the STAR tool with your family. Explain each step and encourage them to try it with you. Have them write down or draw a picture of what they receive. Writing helps with retention.

Going Deeper
Give your child an opportunity to use STAR on their own. Ask them about their experience. Discuss any insights or discoveries they may have had.

I Spy Jesus on TV

Numbers 22:30
And the donkey said to Balaam, "Am I not your donkey, on which you have ridden all your life long to this day?"

Teaching Idea for Parents
God spoke to Balaam through a donkey! Imagine that! His messages to us can come from surprising sources, including various forms of media, including television. Help your child become expectant of hearing from God in surprising and unexpected places, like movies, conversations, cartoons, or even visits to a hobby farm.

Exercises for Families
Choose one of your family's favourite shows and watch it together. As you do, imagine how Jesus would be present in that story. What would he be doing? What words of wisdom or encouragement might Jesus share? Encourage your family to consider the truths that Jesus would want them to see through the storyline.

Going Deeper
Take your child on an outing! We would suggest a favourite nature trail, or even a visit to the library. While there, challenge them to ask, "Jesus, what do you want to show me about yourself?" or "Jesus, where are you and what are you doing?"

I Spy Jesus When I Pray

Jeremiah 33:3
Call to me and I will answer you, and will tell you great and hidden things that you have not known.

Teaching Idea for Parents
Two-way conversations are essential to any relationship. Yet it's easy to forget this in our relationship with God. He speaks most often in the still, small voice (1 Kings 19:12–13), which is a thought that seems like our own but tangibly is not our own. Many of our thoughts are actually Jesus speaking to us! Just as we speak to God, it is equally important to listen to what he is saying to us.

Exercises for Families
Practice hearing God's voice by setting aside some quiet time. Ask Jesus a question and listen for his response. Here's a fun question to start with: "Jesus, what game would you choose to play with me and why?" Share the first thing that comes to mind. Make listening to God's voice a fun experience, something your child looks forward to.

Going Deeper
Set aside time to walk your child through the Whisper Challenge, shared at the back of the book. Be encouraging with even the tiniest progress.

I Spy Jesus When I'm Afraid

Deuteronomy 31:8
It is the Lord who goes before you. He will be with you; he will not leave you or forsake you. Do not fear or be dismayed.

Teaching Idea for Parents
Review the STAR tool, focusing on the emotions of anxiety and fear. Whenever your child encounters these emotions, Jesus has much to say. He does not give us a spirit of fear, but of power and love and self-control (2 Timothy 1:7).

Exercises for Families
Have a conversation with your family about a time when they felt fearful, anxious, worried, or even shy. Go through the steps of STAR and ask Jesus what he is doing or saying in that specific memory.

Going Deeper
If your child has had a nightmare, guide them through STAR. Ask Jesus what he is doing or saying in that dream. Ask him to show your child where he was in the dream. He will open the eyes of their heart to see!

I Spy Jesus in My Dreams

Psalm 16:7
I bless the Lord who gives me counsel; in the night also my heart instructs me.

Teaching Idea for Parents
Even during sleep, when we are unaware of our surroundings, God continues to guide and teach us. He is always present, even in the stillness of the night. He never sleeps but is always working in our lives—and speaking!

Exercises for Families
Encourage your child to create a drawing of a happy dream they remember. Discuss the emotions they felt in the dream. Think about what Jesus might be saying through that dream. Spend some time reflecting on the message or meaning behind it.

Going Deeper
Have your child pray, asking Jesus for further understanding or guidance about other specific dreams. Prayerfully reflect with them.

The Whisper Challenge

This activity will help your child develop their listening skills and sensitivity to Jesus's voice in a playful and engaging way. If at first this is difficult, keep trying. Hearing God's voice can be like learning how to ride a bike or play the piano.

- Find a quiet, comfortable space where you can sit with your child. It could be somewhere in your home, or even a favourite place in nature.

- Encourage your child to close their eyes and take a few deep breaths to relax. This is being still before God (Psalm 46:10).

- Explain that they are going to listen for God's whisper, which is like a soft voice or thought inside their heart. It may seem like their own thought but is tangibly God speaking. 1 Kings 19:12–13 illustrates how God speaks in this fashion. See also Job 26:14.

- Have your child ask God a question. You can be as creative as you want. Here are a couple of suggestions: "What do you want to tell me today?" or "What do you love about me?"

- Give your child a few moments of silence to listen. Have them pay attention to any thoughts, feelings, or images that come to their mind. Remind them that they belong to Jesus and can hear his voice (John 10:27).

- As they listen, the first thoughts that come to your child are key. When we ask for wisdom, we can be sure that God answers (James 1:5–6). Do not doubt!

- After a few minutes, have your child share what they have received. It could be a word, phrase, picture, verse, or even a feeling.

- Discuss what they sensed and how it practically relates to their life. Note: if they don't "hear" anything, remind them that this is okay and sometimes takes practice. Often, asking Jesus a follow-up question is very helpful.

- Have a special journal for them to draw and/or write down what they receive.

God's Comfort Box

Even though I walk through the valley of the shadow of death, I will fear no evil, for you are with me; your rod and your staff, they comfort me. (Psalm 23:4)

This activity will serve as a tangible reminder of this incredible truth: Jesus is always present, bringing comfort and strength, especially during difficult times.

- Find a small box or container that can serve as God's Comfort Box.

- Discuss the importance of knowing that Jesus is present during hard times, bringing comfort, peace, joy, encouragement, wisdom, and strength.

- Decorate the box with markers, stickers, or any other craft supplies.

- Have each family member write or draw about the memory of a difficult situation, challenge, sickness, scary circumstance, or time of need. Choose one. Use a card that is approximately five by seven inches.

- On the back, record how God was present through the difficult time. Include encouraging words from others, special Bible verses, stories of miracles, and especially what God was saying. Remember, God can speak through words, phrases, or pictures. Write down how these things made you feel at the time (for example, comfort, joy, or assurance).

- Place it in God's Comfort Box.

- Whenever someone in the family is going through a difficult time, open God's Comfort Box and take out one of the cards. It will remind your child of Jesus's presence and comfort. This will stir up their expectation that Jesus is present in the current circumstance.

- Use the STAR tool to help your child further process the current challenge. Then pray with them, aligning your prayers to what Jesus is saying. If you want, write this experience on a card and add it to God's Comfort Box.

Author Bio:

Tony and Sara are pastors in Fort St. John, British Columbia and the North American Directors for Church Renewal International. With more than thirty years of pastoral experience, they have an ability to make deep biblical themes, like hearing God's voice, accessible to all, even children. They have published other works, including *Boondock Church: Small Town, Massive Potential* (2019) and *Life on the Inside* (2022), a children's book about the life of the unborn. They have four adult children and eight grandchildren who have formed the laboratory for the teaching in this book. If they ever go MIA, you'll find them in a cabin nestled in the deep wilderness of the Canadian north! To learn more, visit www.boondockpastor.com.

Illustrator Bio:

Tara Brule is a mom of two young adult children who were brought up to recognize the Shepherd's voice. She is an educator, painter, traditional fibre artist, and illustrator who lives on a small farm in northern British Columbia along with her husband, one cat, three horses, a mixed flock of bantam chickens, and a new puppy. Tara also enjoys working in her garden, where she and her family grow vegetables, herbs, cut flowers, and delicious saskatoon berries.

www.ingramcontent.com/pod-product-compliance
Lightning Source LLC
Chambersburg PA
CBHW061400090426
42743CB00002B/83